Co
Little

# Love

Words of warmth and affection
RICHARD DALY

WILLIAM
COLLINS

William Collins
An Imprint of HarperCollins*Publishers*
1 London Bridge Street,
London SE1 9GF

www.williamcollinsbooks.com

9 10 8

First published in Great Britain in
2007 by HarperCollins*Publishers*
This edition 2013

A catalogue record for this book is
available from the British Library

ISBN 978-0-00-752837-0

Printed and bound in China by
RR Donnelley APS LTD

# Introduction

Love – what an endearing word.
It has been the basis for so many poems,
songs, speeches and prose. Through love
human relationships are born, and it is
the golden cord that keeps people
together. It is indeed love that 'makes
the world go round.'

However, what happens when love for
one another is withdrawn, and the power
of its effect reduced? It is disastrous, for
we cannot survive without love. Yet could
it be that we are actually seeing
the evidence of this today?

## Put others first

Be blessed, by blessing other people.

---

For Further Reflection

*Matthew 5:14*

# Fear not

'There is no fear in love, but perfect
love casts out fear.'

For Further Reflection

*1 John 4:18*

# Love is life

The grandest moral and ethical goal of humanity means nothing without love.

---

For Further Reflection

*1 Corinthians 13:1*

# Rest in the arms of God

In extreme assaults of stress God invites
us to rest in his eternal embrace.

For Further Reflection

*Matthew 11:28*

## Love's greatest gift

Through God's great love Christ was
treated as we deserve, so that we can
be treated as he deserves.

For Further Reflection

*John 3:16*

# You're never forgotten

One of the most breathtaking concepts of
scripture is the revelation that God knows
each of us personally, and that we are
constantly on his mind day and night.

---

For Further Reflection

*Psalm 8:4*

# God's love has no boundaries

There is simply no way we can fathom the extent of God's love for us. As the song says, it's so high you can't get over it, so wide you can't get around it, so low you can't get under it.

---

For Further Reflection

*Psalm 139:1–2*

# An unconditional love

God continues to love us even when we
don't feel the same towards him.

---

For Further Reflection

*Romans 5:8*

## God's on your case!

Never assume that God is silent or inactive simply because it seems we do not hear from him. Be assured, he is silently working on your case.

For Further Reflection

*Psalm 37:34*

## You're never alone!

The Lord doesn't always solve our problems instantly. Sometimes he permits us to walk through the 'valley of the shadow of death.' But he is there with us, even in our darkest hours. We can never escape his endless love.

---

For Further Reflection

*Psalm 73:23*

*Psalm 23*

## Cast your cares on him

God hears the faintest cry of the sick,
the lonely, the bereaved and the depressed
of the world. He cares deeply about
each one.

For Further Reflection

*Psalm 40:1*

# An ever-present friend

God's heart is tenderly drawn towards the
downtrodden and the defeated. He knows
your name, and sees every tear.

---

For Further Reflection

*Psalm 34:18*

## Be comforted

'The Lord is close to the broken-hearted,
and saves those who are crushed in spirit.'

---

For Further Reflection

*Psalm 34:18*

# The silent protector

We will never know how often the Lord
quietly protects us, directs or leads us.
He is an ever-present companion.

For Further Reflection
*Psalm 46:1*

# Only trust him

When we submit to the will of the Lord we can say with confidence that in all things God works for the good of them who love him, who have been called according to his purpose.

For Further Reflection

*James 1:17*

# Not our time, but his

While God's purposes and plans are
different from ours, he is infinitely just,
and his timing is always perfect.

---

For Further Reflection
*2 Samuel 7:28–29*

# From test to testimony

God wants to use the lessons from
your experiences of adversity, to encourage
others going through the same thing.

---

For Further Reflection

*Genesis 12:2*

# To know God is to experience him

It's during those periods where your
faith has been challenged that you get
a better understanding of who God is,
and the extent of his love.

---

For Further Reflection

*Psalm 91:4*

# Watch your moods

Establish your spiritual foundation not on fluctuating emotions but on the authority of God's written word. God's love never changes.

---

For Further Reflection

*Malachi 3:6*

## Let go, let God

We are assured in scripture that we are never left to fight our battles alone. That is great news for all who are weary and burdened.

For Further Reflection

*1 Samuel 17:47*
*2 Chronicles 20:15*

# Spread love

'As I have loved you, so you must
love one another.'

---

For Further Reflection

*John 15:12, 17*
*Hebrew 13:1*

## Put first things first

'I may have all knowledge, and understand all secrets. I may have all the faith needed to move mountains – but if I have no love, I am nothing.'

For Further Reflection
*1 Corinthians 13*

# Be a conqueror

'Who shall separate us from the love of Christ? Shall trouble or hardship or persecution or famine or nakedness or danger or sword? No, in all these things we are more than conquerors through him who loves us.'

---

For Further Reflection

*Romans 8: 35–37*

# He's got your back!

God's love for us is a protective love.
He says, 'He that touches you, touches
the apple of my eye.'

---

For Further Reflection

*Zechariah 2:8*

## You are priceless

The price paid for us was imaginably high –
the blood of Jesus Christ. Now we belong to
him. That ought to put a smile on our faces.

---

For Further Reflection

*John 3:16, 17*
*1 Corinthians 6:20*

## Losing to win

We often think of love as giving, but
sometimes love involves taking away
something that would not be best.

---

For Further Reflection

*Job 1:21*

# Avoid the myth

Contrary to popular opinion, God doesn't sit in heaven with his jaws clenched, hand in a fist and a deep frown on his face.

---

For Further Reflection

*Exodus 34:6, 7*

# Lay down your burdens

Our problem is that we hold on to our
worries and anxieties. The Bible says
'Cast your cares upon him, for he
cares for you.'

---

For Further Reflection

*1 Peter 5:7*

# God is who you need him to be

In God we have a Lord and a shepherd:
a Lord who can place a hundred billion stars
in space, who is so mind-numbingly mighty;
yet who can come to us as a shepherd
and touch us with the gentleness of
a mother's hand.

---

For Further Reflection

*Psalm 23:1*

# Make the change

What's blocking you from experiencing God's love? Find out as soon as possible, and refuse to live another day without that love in your life.

---

For Further Reflection

**Romans 5:5**

## Turn it over to Jesus

What matters to you, matters to God.
There's no problem so insignificant that he
doesn't want you to tell him about it. What's
important to you is important to God.

---

For Further Reflection

*Hebrews 13:22*
*Hebrews 13:5*

## Let God lead

If you believe that God has a unique plan
for your life and loves you unconditionally,
you will abandon yourself to him in
trust, knowing that in the end 'all will go
well' for you.

---

For Further Reflection
*Jeremiah 29:11*

## Experience freedom

Whatever you refuse to forgive, you relive.
It robs you of the joy of loving and of being
loved in return. Unforgiveness is an umbilical
cord that keeps you tied to the past. When
you forgive, you cut that cord.

---

For Further Reflection
*Ephesians 4:32*

# There's hope for you

You who have been abused, abandoned, betrayed, or feel as if you never measure up: God says to you, 'I have loved you with an everlasting love; I have drawn you with loving-kindness. I will build you up again.'

---

For Further Reflection

*Jeremiah 31:3, 4*

## Rise to the challenge

Loving others does not mean much if we only love the people we choose to, based on our terms and conditions. But loving those who are different from us in personality, culture, race, and loving them in spite of their difference is the real challenge!

---

For Further Reflection

*John 13:34*

## Release your potential

Jesus does not penalise us for our past,
or label us. Knowing the worst about us,
he still sees the best. That's what he
expects us to do for others, too!

---

For Further Reflection

*Ephesians 5:2*

## Choose to love

Love is a choice, not a mood, a magic
feeling or a reaction, but a choice.

---

For Further Reflection

*1 Peter 2:4*
*Isaiah 43:1*

# Worship in spirit and truth

Our worship to God ought to be a total expression of our gratitude and praise to the one who loved us when we were hopeless, destitute, lonely, fearful. Who filled us with his peace, wrapped us in his own identity, and gave us a place of honour.

---

For Further Reflection

*Psalm 113:3*

## Esteem others highly

Never let your own suffering blind you to the needs of those around you. Jesus was more concerned with other people's needs than his own. We should take our cue from him.

For Further Reflection

*Philippians 2:3, 4*

# Be a vessel of love

God is looking for people he can use as
a vessel to reach out to love other people.
Will you be one?

---

For Further Reflection
*2 Peter 2:21*

# From selfish to selfless love

Modern thinking says 'I'll love you if you meet my needs.' That's selfish. True love focuses on the needs of the other person.

---

For Further Reflection

*Ephesians 5:25–27*

## True love part 1

'Love is patient and kind, never jealous or envious, never boastful or proud, never haughty or selfish or rude. Love does not demand its own way. It is not irritable or touchy. It does not hold grudges, and will hardly ever notice when others do it wrong'.

For Further Reflection

*1 Corinthians 13:4, 5*

# True love part 2

When you love someone you will be loyal to them no matter what the cost, you will always believe in them, always expect the best, and always stand your ground defending them.

---

For Further Reflection

*1 Corinthians 13:6, 7*

# Love the unloving

Avoid the trap of self-righteousness, and act with humility and grace when you encounter someone whose lifestyle makes you uncomfortable. Begin to see them not through your preconceptions but as someone loved by God, and in need of the same grace you received.

---

For Further Reflection

*1 John 4:8*

# Value yourself, value others

Good marriages, relationships and friendships are all based on Christ's golden rule. 'Whatever you want someone to do to you, do also to them.'

---

For Further Reflection

*Matthew 7:12*

# Love is a lasting journey

Against popular opinion, Love doesn't 'make the world go round': Love is what makes the ride worthwhile.

---

For Further Reflection

*Song of Solomon 8:7*

## Learn from your past

Every experience you have had, from the moment you were born until now, has made you who you are today. Use these experiences to cultivate your love.

---

For Further Reflection
*Romans 8:28*

# A word of affirmation

One of the most beautiful passages in
scripture is found in Isaiah: 'You are mine.
When you pass through the waters, I will be
with you. When you walk through the fire
you will not be burned; you are precious and
honoured in my sight. I love you.'

---

For Further Reflection

*Isaiah 43:1–4*

# To be loved, love

Our attitude toward others determines
their attitude towards us. Smile at people
and they will smile back. Show acts of
love, and they will reciprocate.

---

For Further Reflection

*Proverbs 23:7*

# Be transformed by love

God likes to take the lost, the least and the
lowest and make something beautiful of
them. If you feel like you are one of the
above, let God do what he likes to do best
and make you an object of beauty.

For Further Reflection

*Isaiah 1:18*

## Check your motives

True love will never ask of a person anything that will devalue them, or disassociate them from God's will.

---

For Further Reflection

*Philippians 4:8*

# Respect your loved one

If 'God is love' the reverse must also
be true: 'love is godly.'

---

For Further Reflection

*Amos 5:15*

## Don't be fooled by feelings

Someone said, 'Love is a feeling you feel
when you feel you're going to feel something
you've never felt before.' Fortunately, real
love doesn't depend on just feelings.

---

For Further Reflection

*1 Corinthians 13:7, 8*

## Love in three words

Many poems have been written and many songs sung, all trying to define the one word, love. One dictionary uses 27 words. The Bible defines it in just three, 'God is love.'

---

For Further Reflection

*1 John 4:6*

# With God, you can't lose

God's love to us is unfailing – your name is engraved on the palm of his hand. He knows you better than you know yourself, your sins of yesterday and of tomorrow are before his eyes; yet the verdict is still, 'I love you.'

---

For Further Reflection
*Psalm 103:11*

# Memorise John 3:16

This verse is perhaps the greatest expression of love ever: 'For God so loved the world, that he gave his only begotten son, that whosoever believes in him should not perish, but have everlasting life.'

---

For Further Reflection

*John 3:16*

# Let love change you

Some think, 'If I try, I can change my partner.'
Don't use your love to try to change your
partner, use your love to change yourself!

---

For Further Reflection

*Romans 12:3*

## Wait on him

'And we know that in all things, God works
for the good of those who love him, who
have been called according to his purpose.'

For Further Reflection

*Romans 8:28*

# Be there

When someone is hurting, the most loving thing to do is simply to be there. Though you have nothing to offer except your presence, that speaks louder than words.

---

For Further Reflection

*2 Corinthians 1:4*

## Live unselfishly

Give without expecting in return, forgive
even though you are not forgiven. Share,
though no one says thank you. This
is love in action.

---

For Further Reflection

*Luke 6:35*

## It's OK to love yourself

To love yourself is not about pride, but an appreciation of who you are in Christ. Before we can love others, we have to learn to love ourselves.

---

For Further Reflection

*Matthew 22:39*
*James 2:8*

# Loving can be difficult

The greatest sacrifice we make is
choosing to love those who are not
easy to love.

---

For Further Reflection

*Matthew 5:44*
*Luke 6:27*

## Be childlike

Children have a natural way of spontaneously expressing their feelings of love. If there's any virtue in regression, that could be it.

For Further Reflection
*Mark 10:15*

# Love never ends

The fact that love never fails, means it never gives up, nor permits itself to be hindered or defeated by evil. It is constant, immovable.

---

For Further Reflection

*Jeremiah 31:3*

# Keep God's law

The Ten Commandments can be summed up in one word – love. Love for God, and love for our neighbour. God says, if you love me, keep my commandments!

---

For Further Reflection

*1 John 5:2*
*John 15:10*

# Guard against selfishness

By nature, we are often 'takers'. Biblical love involves making a conscious decision to be 'givers', asking 'What can I do to serve you?' rather than, 'What's in it for me?'

---

For Further Reflection

*Mark 10:45*

# Accept the rain, and shine

A love that is 'enduring' weathers
the storm of life.

---

For Further Reflection

*Psalm 107:29*
*Isaiah 25:4*

# Love conquers all

'There is no difficulty that enough love can not conquer; no disease that enough love will not heal no door that enough love will not open no gulf that enough love will not bridge no wall that enough love cannot bring down!'

*Emmet Fox*

---

For Further Reflection

**Romans 8:37**

# See yourself as lovable

Much happiness is achieved when
there's the conviction that you are loved
in spite of yourself.

For Further Reflection

*Proverbs 10:12*

# Give love, get love

'If you want to be loved, love
and be loveable.'

*Benjamin Franklin*

---

For Further Reflection

***Romans 13:8***

# Express love creatively

There are many inexpensive ways to tell
the one you love how much you care –
write a poem (it doesn't have to rhyme),
plan a surprise lunch, hide love notes
around the house. Be creative!

---

For Further Reflection

*Song of Solomon 4:1–16*

# Get ready for a surprise

'No eye has seen, no ear has heard, no mind has conceived, what God has prepared for those who love him.'

---

For Further Reflection

*1 Corinthians 2:9*

## Express your love today

The revealed instinctive desire of many when
facing death is to call a loved one, to say
'I love you'. But why wait until such a crisis?

---

For Further Reflection
*Song of Solomon 7:10*

# Make a commitment

True love is not a feeling by which we are
overwhelmed. It is a thought-out decision,
by which we are committed.

---

For Further Reflection
*Psalm 18:1*

# Love your enemies

It is natural to love those who love us. It is supernatural to love those who hate us.

---

For Further Reflection

*Proverbs 8:17*
*Hosea 14:4*

## An impartial love

There is nothing you can do to make
God love you more. There is nothing you
can do to make God love you less.

---

For Further Reflection

*John 15:13*

## Let Christ fill you

By its nature, human love is conditional.
Only through Christ in us can we produce
agape (unconditional love), only he can
fulfil us in joy, peace, and compassion.

---

For Further Reflection

*2 Corinthians 5:14*

# A motive of love

'It is not how much you do, but how much
love you put into the doing, that matters.'

*Mother Teresa*

---

For Further Reflection
**Psalm 17:17**

# Love seeks not its own

'Love consists in desiring to give what
is our own to another, and feeling that
delight as our own.'

*Emanuel Swedenborg*

For Further Reflection

*Micah 6:8*

# Create a loving atmosphere

Every house where love abides and
friendship is a guest, is surely a true home.

For Further Reflection
*Mark 3:25*

## Seize the moment

'I shall pass through the world but once,
any good that I can do or act of kindness,
let me do it now, let me not deter or neglect
it, for I shall not pass this way again.'

*Stephen Grellett*

---

For Further Reflection
**Psalm 118:24**

# Cherish loving memories

Nothing can erase those precious moments of love known within your life. These treasures belong to you, and are to be cherished for the rest of your life.

---

For Further Reflection

*Psalm 105:5*
*Song of Solomon 1:4*

## Enjoy your life

'The more you give, the more you get. The more you laugh, the less you fret. The more you do unselfishly, the more you live abundantly.'

*B Kent*

---

For Further Reflection

*Luke 6:38*

## Be blessed to bless

Each of us has been entrusted with
certain gifts to steward for each day.
Let us use them well; life is ours for
such a brief span of time.

_____

For Further Reflection
*Matthew 5:16*

## Pray with love

If love is the greatest force in the world,
and prayer the mightiest force in the world,
then when we pray in love we are working
with a power that can move the world.

---

For Further Reflection

*James 5:16*

# Remember the golden rule

Show love to others, as you would have them show love to you. This is the golden rule of love.

---

For Further Reflection

*1 John 4:19*
*John 15:12*

## Watch your reflections

Life is like a mirror: if you frown at it, it frowns back. If you smile, it returns the greeting.

---

For Further Reflection

*Galatians 6:7*

## Get rid of hate

'When Jesus said "love your enemy", he meant every word of it. We never get rid of an enemy by meeting hate with hate. We get rid of an enemy by getting rid of enmity.'

*Martin Luther King*

---

For Further Reflection

*1 John 4:18*
*Luke 6:27*

# The essential ingredient

What is important in life is knowing
how to give and receive love.

---

For Further Reflection
*1 Peter 2:17*

# Claim your inheritance

As God's beloved child, you are a member
of the royal family of the king of heaven. You
are highly esteemed and greatly honoured.
You are an heir to God's kingdom, and
have direct access to the throne room
of God. You're royalty!

---

For Further Reflection
*1 Peter 2:9*

# Love's not a fairytale

A truism of love is that it ends happily ever
after – yet true love has no ending.

---

For Further Reflection

*Psalm 34:12*

# Grow in love

Contrary to popular belief, we never 'fall' in love, but 'grow' in a greater understanding and appreciation of what it really is.

For Further Reflection
*2 Peter 3:18*

## Love sees all

Love is not 'blind': it sees more, not less,
but because it sees more, it chooses
to see less.

---

For Further Reflection

*Romans 5:8*

# Don't be deceived

Many people confuse infatuation with love.
One is a temporary, changing emotion,
the other is a giving, permanent, principled
decision. Don't be fooled!

---

For Further Reflection

*Proverbs 17:17*

# Look for the open door

When the door of happiness closes, another door opens. However, often we look so long at the closed door that we don't see the one which has been opened for us.

---

For Further Reflection
*Revelation 3:8*

## See through their eyes

Always put yourself in others' shoes. If you
feel them rubbing at you painfully, they
probably hurt them too!

---

For Further Reflection

*Romans 12:14–21*

## Learn to be patient

To love someone is to let them just be themselves, and not to seek to change them into our own image. Otherwise we love only the reflection of ourselves we find in them.

---

For Further Reflection

*Philippians 3:21*
*1 Corinthians 15:51*

## Be content

The happiest people don't necessarily have the best of everything, they simply make the most of everything that comes their way.

---

For Further Reflection

*Hebrews 13:5*
*Philippians 4:11*

## Express appreciation

Never miss an opportunity to let those who
are essential to your life know how much you
love, appreciate, and think of them each day.

---

For Further Reflection
*Ephesians 5:20*

## Just one word for love

We say we love our spouse, our children,
and in the same breath we say that we
love fried eggs. Don't let language
confuse your understanding.

---

For Further Reflection
*1 John 4:7*

# Love can do wonders

'I love you not only for what you are, but
for what I am when I am with you. I love you
not only for what you have made yourself,
but for what you are making me.'

---

For Further Reflection

**Ephesians 4:15**

# Let God fill your emptiness

We all have a void in our lives that needs to be filled with love. Often human love falls short of filling this, but this void can be filled through the love of God. Open your heart to him today.

For Further Reflection

*Ephesians 3:19*

## Bought with a price

A high price was paid by God to show
his love for us. Through Christ, that love
is freely available.

---

For Further Reflection

*Hebrews 12:2*

# When love hurts

When we love someone, we take them
into our hearts. That is why it hurts so much
when we lose someone we love – because
we lose a part of ourselves.

---

For Further Reflection

*Revelation 21:4*

## Avoid possessiveness

'Possessive' love cannot be true love
at all: in fact, it is an act of selfishness.
Love ought to respect a person too
much to dominate them.

---

For Further Reflection

*John 5:42*

# Let God repair the hurt

Have you been let down by someone
you love? Jesus is 'very close to the broken-
hearted, and very near to those who
are crushed in spirit.'

---

For Further Reflection

*Psalm 34:18*

## Learn from children

Learn to express your love freely and without inhibition. Take a lesson from children: they do it all the time.

For Further Reflection

*Matthew 19:14*

# Cover hatred with love

Hate has a reason for everything.
But love is un-reasonable.

---

For Further Reflection

*Amos 5:15*
*Luke 6:27*

# Follow your instincts

The moment a child is born, their natural instinctive need is for love. When death stares you in the eyes, the last natural instinctive need is love.

For Further Reflection
*Isaiah 66:13*

# Soften up!

No matter how tough people's exterior may be, we all need to love and to be loved.

---

For Further Reflection

**Romans 5:5**

## Know your reason for living

There are three questions of value in life.
What is sacred? What is worth living for?
And what is worth dying for? The answer
to each is the same: only love.

---

For Further Reflection

*John 15:13*

# Give to receive

Love is quite something: if you give it
away, it comes right back to you.

For Further Reflection

*Matthew 10:8*
*Luke 6:38*

# Never feel you're unloved!

What motivates you to live another day?
It must be love. What motivates you not
to want to live another day? The false
perception that you are not loved.
But God always loves you!

---

For Further Reflection

*2 Peter 3:9*
*John 3:16*

## You deserve it

Those who need to be loved the most,
are those who deserve it the least.

_____

For Further Reflection
*Luke 7:47*

# Give hope to a life

If someone tells you that 'nobody loves
them', endeavour to prove them wrong.

---

For Further Reflection

*Genesis 4:9*

# Be amazed by grace

The amazing thing about God's love for
us is that he accepts us just as we are!

---

For Further Reflection

*Psalm 103:10*
*Roman 4:7*

# Don't neglect yourself

If we are committed to loving others,
we must also treat ourselves with
the same love.

---

For Further Reflection
*John 3:2*

# Accept God's forgiveness

Forgiveness is a fruit of love. And it also involves learning to forgive ourselves.

For Further Reflection
*Psalm 91:1–13*

# Confession is good for the soul

When a person accepts the forgiveness of God, they are exposing themselves to the greatest therapeutic power in the world. It could save years of physical and spiritual illness.

For Further Reflection

*Luke 23:34*
*Luke 6:37*

## Give it up

By handing over your problem to God,
we can experience the power of emotional
release, a very real enhancer of the
immune system.

---

For Further Reflection
*Psalm 55:22*

# Unstoppable

'Many waters cannot quench love.'

---

For Further Reflection

*Song of Solomon 8:7*

# Be faithful in little things

One source of happiness is to find
time to make one small act of service each
day. Only those who love to give, have
really learned to live life.

---

For Further Reflection

*1 John 3:18*

# Be open-minded

We all need to learn not to be quick
to judge, or quick to condemn.

---

For Further Reflection

*Romans 14:13*

# Hug someone today

Hugging is all natural. It's organic, naturally
sweet, no pesticides or preservatives.
No artificial ingredients and 100 per cent
wholesome. Doesn't that sound nutritious?

---

For Further Reflection

**Romans 12:9, 10**

# Think lovely thoughts

'Whatsoever things are true, whatsoever things are lovely – think on these things.'

For Further Reflection
*Philippians 4:8*

## Write a love letter

Expressing your love to someone in writing
allows you to choose the choicest words
that reflect the inner sentiments of the heart.
Once inscribed, it can be treasured for life.

---

For Further Reflection
*Job 19:23*
*Proverbs 3:3*

# Read his love story

The Song of Solomon contains the
most loving descriptive passages. Read a
passage today, and get some tips.

<hr>

For Further Reflection

*Song of Solomon 4:1–5*

## Meditate on nature

Look around you: there are hundreds
of ways in which God is telling you how
much he cares. He says, 'Be still and
know that I am God.'

---

For Further Reflection

*Psalm 46:10*

## Store precious moments

Loving memories always bring a welcome smile. By creating such moments today, you'll always have something to look back on.

For Further Reflection
*Psalm 139:17*

# Be a source of hope

Giving is the secret of a healthy life
– not necessarily giving money, but
encouragement, sympathy
and understanding.

---

For Further Reflection

*Deuteronomy 1:39*
*Deuteronomy 3:28*

# Maintain your friendships

True friendships do not come by
chance. Each one is infinitely precious.
They are a source of life's lasting joys,
so appreciate them.

---

For Further Reflection

***Proverbs 17:17***

## Only ask

As long as it draws you closer to him rather than pulling away, whatever you need, if you trust God, he will supply it.

---

For Further Reflection

*John 14:13*
*Luke 11:9*

# Spend time alone

There are great benefits to be had from
a time of solitude. A brief hour on your
own before returning to the world
relaxed and refreshed.

---

For Further Reflection

*Psalm 23:2*

# Let children see love in you

Give your children a home wherein
Love's fires are lit and never grow dim.
A place where children may always know
That they with their pleasures and
troubles may go.

For Further Reflection
*Psalm 127:3*

# One family

If God is our heavenly father, and
we are his children, that makes us equal.
We are all brothers and sisters of the
same one family.

---

For Further Reflection
*Galatians 3:28*

## Lead by example

Making children feel loved and wanted is
the primary aim of all parents. The simplest
and most direct way to do this, is to tell
them so, many times, day after day.

---

For Further Reflection

*Proverbs 22:6*

# Trust in prayer

Prayer is the answer to every problem in life. It puts us in tune with divine wisdom, which knows how to adjust everything perfectly.

For Further Reflection

*Luke 18:1*
*1 Timothy 2:8*

## Choose your mood

It takes no greater effort to be happy
everyday than it does to be miserable.

---

For Further Reflection

*Proverbs 16:20*
*Proverbs 3:13*

## Send an encouraging card

What can dispel thoughts of despondency
better than receiving a letter from a friend?
What we write can say so much.

---

For Further Reflection

*Luke 1:1–4*

# Be hopeful

'Yesterday is always a dream
Tomorrow is only a vision
But today well lived
Makes yesterday a dream of happiness
And tomorrow a dream of hope.'

*Kalidasa*

---

For Further Reflection

*Matthew 6:25–34*

## Let today be your day

Today is your day and mine, so let
us search for the lovely things.

---

For Further Reflection

*John 16:24*

## Let God heal you

In truth it is difficult to love someone who has caused you much hurt and pain. In such a case, present yourself to God to heal those wounds so you can love again.

---

For Further Reflection

*Matthew 5:11, 12*

## Live to love

To live is to love, and to love is to live.

---

For Further Reflection
*1 John 4:16*

# Love to be loved

If you wish to be loved, love.

---

For Further Reflection
*1 John 3:17, 18*

## Give yourself

Love, above all, is the gift of oneself.

---

For Further Reflection

*James 1:17*

# The greatest of all

'And now these three remain: faith, hope
and love. But the greatest of these is love.'

---

For Further Reflection

*1 Corinthians 13:13*

# Don't rush ahead

We live in a fast-paced world where we have come to expect instantaneous results. God doesn't operate that way: he is not bound by our time.

---

For Further Reflection

*Acts 1:7*

# Seek his righteousness

'Every work of love brings a person
face to face with God.'

*Mother Teresa*

---

For Further Reflection
**1 Corinthians 13:12**

# Find a secret garden

A beautiful garden is a peaceful spot
where you can stop to reflect and catch a
glimpse of life's deeper meaning. Visit one
today, and be enthralled.

---

For Further Reflection

*John 18:1*

# Love is...

There are many metaphors for love.
Yet no human words can really define it.

---

For Further Reflection
*1 Peter 1:8*

## Always give a positive word

One way of experiencing love is through
receiving compliments. Yet they are
'biodegradable': they dissolve over time
after we receive them. That's why we can
always use another.

---

For Further Reflection
*1 Thessalonians 5:11*

## Love gives vitality

When you think you're in love, you don't go off your food; on the contrary, your appetite for good things is enhanced.

---

For Further Reflection
*Song of Solomon 2:10–17*

## Loving when it's not reciprocated

Giving someone your love is not an assurance that they'll love you back. Don't demand love in return, wait for it to grow in their heart. If it doesn't, be content that it's growing in yours.

---

For Further Reflection

*John 15:18*
*1 John 3:13, 15*